If Monet painted a MONSTER

Written by **AMY NEWBOLD**
Pictures by **GREG NEWBOLD**

TILBURY HOUSE PUBLISHERS, THOMASTON, MAINE

If you painted a monster,

it might have three glowing eyes . . .

. . . or sharp, pointy teeth.

Your monster might
hide under the bed . . .

. . . or have big, furry feet.

Artists paint monsters
in many ways.

Edward Hopper's monster lurks in the shadows,
watching diners eat a late-night snack.

In the gathering gloom, James Whistler's monster waits in her creaking chair.

She is watching, watching, watching as the fog rolls in.

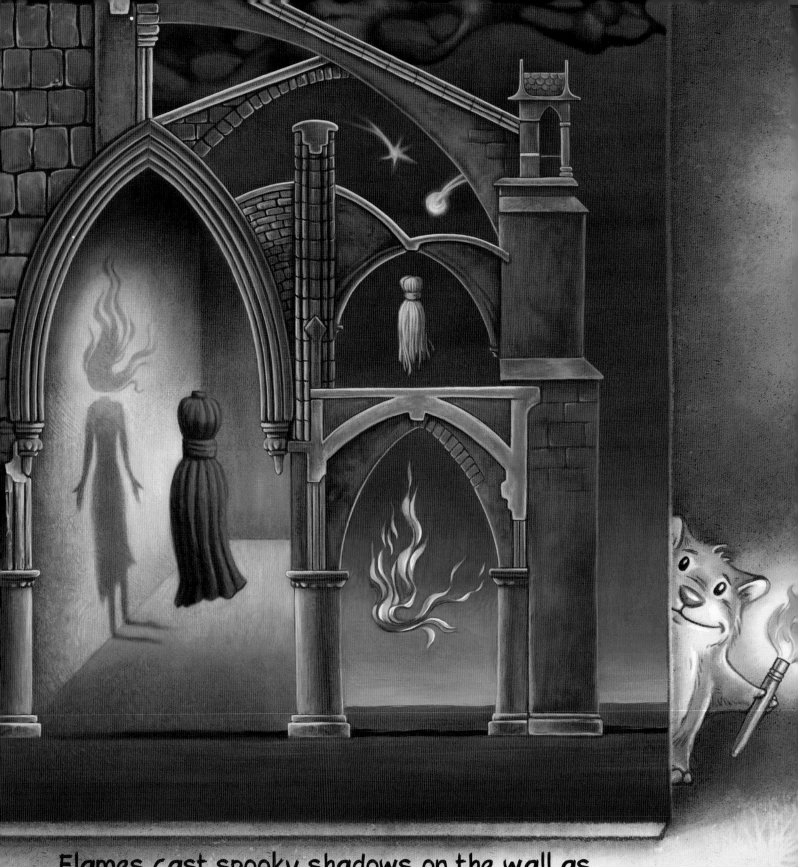

Flames cast spooky shadows on the wall as Dorothea Tanning's monster takes a midnight stroll.

M. C. Escher's creatures creep up and down, around and around.

Rattle, rattle, shriek! Jean-Michel Basquiat's monster howls at sunset.

Giuseppe Arcimboldo's monster is ready for a costume party, festooned in his vegetable disguise.

How many specters does
René Magritte's invisible man reveal?

Henri Rousseau's creatures hunt slithering snakes in the jungle.

With bold, slashing strokes, Franz Kline's monster leaves his mark.

Would you play with Frida Kahlo's little monster?
She brought you a mask.

Skittering, screeching, twisting, and tumbling, Robert Thompson's monsters circle and stomp through the forest.

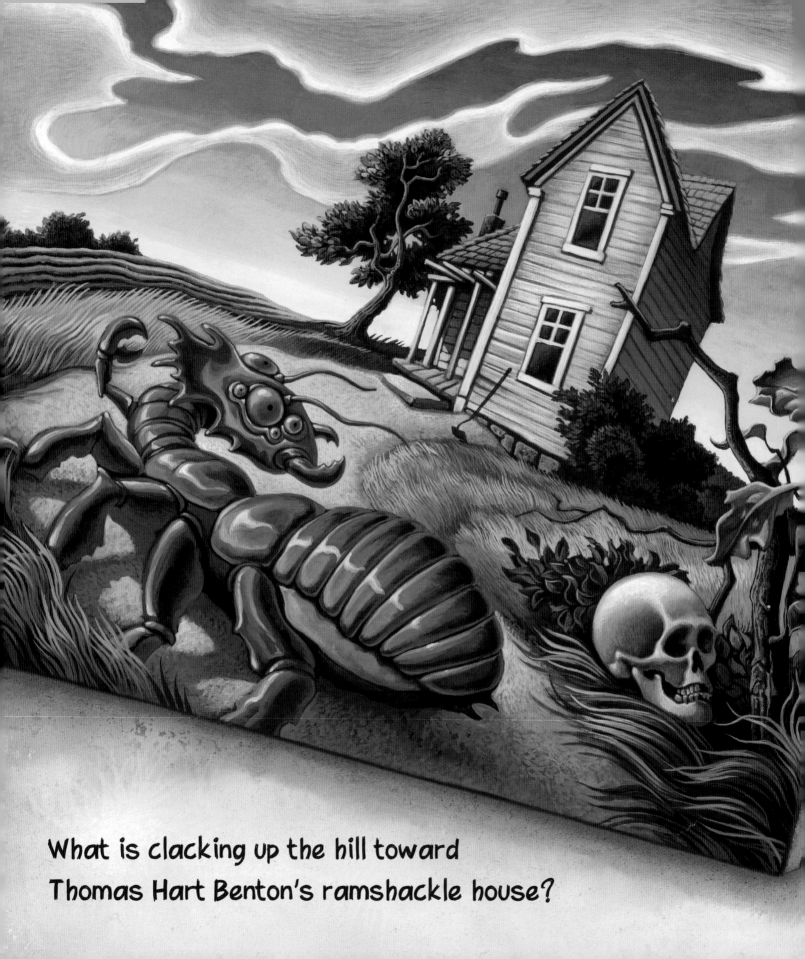

What is clacking up the hill toward
Thomas Hart Benton's ramshackle house?

Flicking their wrists and kicking their heels, the monsters of Henri de Toulouse-Lautrec perform their danse macabre.

Here is Helen Frankenthaler's Frankenstein. Some assembly is required.

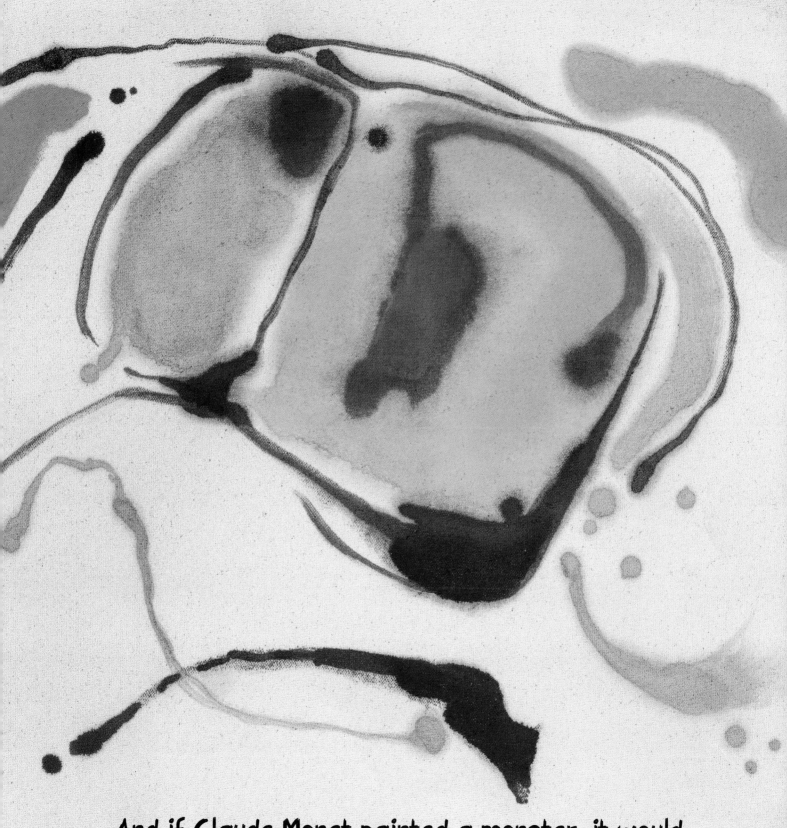

And if Claude Monet painted a monster, it would emerge from the misty water lilies like . . .

What will your monster look like?

Copy this page and make your own.

Meet the Artists

The artists in this book came from all walks of life. While some received formal art training, others were self-taught. All of them persevered through challenges to develop a strong artistic voice. Greg's paintings were inspired by each artist's unique style. When he has based an illustration on a specific masterpiece, that painting is mentioned in the information below.

 **Edward Hopper** (1882–1967) was over six feet tall by the time he was twelve. He loved sketching, painting, and sailing as a boy. Born in New York, Edward began his art career as an illustrator. When designing a painting, Hopper made several sketches before deciding which composition to paint. His work is known for strong lines and his stark use of light. People in Hopper's paintings seem disconnected from their surroundings. One of his most famous paintings, *The Nighthawks*, shows lonely customers eating in a diner. As an American Realist, he painted everyday scenes. Hopper said, "All I ever wanted to do is paint sunlight on the side of a wall."

 **James Abbot McNeill Whistler** (1834–1903) was born in Massachusetts but moved to Russia in 1843 to join his father, who had been hired to design a railroad from St. Petersburg to Moscow for Czar Nicholas I. James was often unruly but always enjoyed taking art lessons. In Paris and London, he painted ships and river scenes. As his work developed, he wanted to create art for art's sake. *Arrangement in Grey and Black No. 1* (also known as *Whistler's Mother*) was his breakthrough piece. Whistler was a transitional artist between Impressionism and Abstraction. He didn't think an artist had to copy nature; he said that an artist "is born to pick and choose . . . elements [so] that the results may be beautiful," just as musicians arrange musical notes into melodies.

 **Dorothea Tanning** (1910–2012) once said, "I learned early to use my imagination and drew and painted a world of my own." Born in rural Illinois, she knew by age ten that she wanted to be an artist. Dorothea's early paintings are Surrealist, depicting scenes from her dreams with a meticulous technique. She read gothic novels and liked putting mysterious elements in paintings such as *A Mrs. Radcliffe Called Today*. As her career progressed, Tanning painted energetic abstracts in vivid color, formed soft sculptures, created costume and set designs for ballets and plays, made lithographs, and wrote poetry.

Paul Cézanne (1839–1906) studied law in France, according to his father's wish, but gave it up to pursue an art career in Paris. He developed a technique of using color to create form, particularly in his still-life paintings. Cézanne often painted outside and made several pictures of Mont Sainte-Victoire, a mountain in southern France, but his paintings were repeatedly rejected by the famous Salon exhibition in Paris. Despite criticism and disappointments, Paul continued to develop his artistic style. He said, "Painting certainly means more to me than everything else in the world. I think my mind becomes clearer when I am in the presence of nature."

Maurits Cornelis Escher (1898–1972) loved music and carpentry as a child in the Netherlands. He began studying architecture but was encouraged by a teacher to become a graphic artist instead. Maurits learned to make wood-cuts and lithographs. He enjoyed changing perspectives and creating optical surprises. In a series of drawings that included his famous *Reptiles*, Escher created patterns of interlocking shapes called tessellations. He said, "My subjects are often playful. Are you sure that a floor can't also be a ceiling? Are you absolutely certain that you go up when walking up a staircase?" The perspective-bending brilliance of M.C. Escher (as he came to be known) continues to amaze people today.

Jean-Michel Basquiat (1960–1988) was born in Brooklyn, New York, to a Haitian father and a Puerto Rican mother. Jean-Michel had no art training beyond visiting museums as a child. He created street art before leaving the graffiti world behind to focus on painting. His bold, colorful works were influenced by African primitive art, Andy Warhol prints, Leonardo da Vinci drawings, and Pablo Picasso paintings. Using collage techniques, paint, and oil sticks, Jean-Michel created art on everything from canvas to refrigerators. His paintings made statements about racism, economic inequality, and other social issues and often included words and symbols. Basquiat said, "I like kids' work more than work by real artists any day." He was only twenty-seven when he died.

Giuseppe Arcimboldo (1526/7–1593) was born in Milan, Italy. He made stained glass and frescoes before going to work for the Hapsburg court in Austria. During his twenty-five years with the Hapsburgs, Arcimboldo enjoyed a great deal of creative freedom. He planned festivals, designed costumes, and wrote poetry for three emperors. Giuseppe used his knowledge of the natural world in his paintings, and his portrait of Rudolf II is comprised of vegetables. Some of his paintings are "reversible." A painting that appeared to be a bowl of produce, when turned upside down, revealed a portrait of a man wearing a hat. Through the years, Arcimboldo's work was largely forgotten until he was rediscovered by the Surrealists, who admired his visual whimsy. He has been called the "grandfather of Surrealism."

René Magritte (1898–1967), an avid moviegoer as a child in Belgium, once put a cinema hero in a painting. René began taking drawing lessons at age twelve. As he developed artistically, he painted ideas rather than traditional representations of people and places. Like many Surrealist painters, he created an alternative reality in his artwork. Magritte's paintings might show birds emerging from leaves, a night landscape with a day sky, or a door with an irregularly shaped opening as in *The Unexpected Answer*. He said, "Art evokes the mystery without which the world would not exist."

Henri Julien Félix Rousseau (1844–1910) excelled in art and music when young but didn't begin painting until age forty, after working for years as a tax collector in Paris. At first his paintings were poorly reviewed, but that didn't stop Henri. He often visited the Jardin des Plantes in Paris to gather inspiration for his fantastical jungle paintings. As a self-taught artist, he had a unique style and a natural sense of color. While his figurative paintings are often called Naïve, his jungle paintings have a more decorative, stylized quality. Rousseau differed from the Impressionists not only in brush strokes but also in utilizing black paint in his works. His style contributed to the development of modern art. Henri said he had "no teacher but nature," and that let his artistic voice shine.

Franz Kline (1910–1962) grew up in rural Pennsylvania and loved illustration from an early age. He studied painting and drawing before moving to New York, where he was introduced to abstract painting by Willem de Kooning. Franz made small black-and-white paintings until he used de Kooning's projector to enlarge his pictures. Then, inspired by a new vision, he began making large, Abstract Expressionist paintings with energetic lines and tonal contrasts. Kline often painted with house paint because he liked how the paint flowed and the way it dried. While some of his art is quite colorful, he is noted for his layered black-and-white paintings. Kline said, "I paint not the things I see but the feelings they arouse in me."

 **Frida Kahlo** (1907–1954) was a Mexican artist who suffered illnesses and injuries in her youth that plagued her throughout her life. Frida found relief in painting and expressed her struggles in her art. Over one-third of her paintings are self-portraits. She often used bright colors and symbols representative of her culture. In 1938, Frida painted *Girl with Death Mask,* depicting a young girl with masks and flowers commonly used in celebrating the Day of the Dead in Mexico. The subtitle of that painting, *She Plays Alone*, is particularly poignant, as Kahlo often experienced loneliness. She said, "I paint self-portraits because I am so often alone, because I am the person I know best."

 **Robert Louis Thompson** (1937–1966) was an African-American artist from Kentucky. When he was thirteen his father died in a car accident, and Bob painted to cope with his grief and depression. Later he moved to New York to be an artist. He studied Italian Renaissance painters in Europe and went on to create his own style, combining themes from the old masters with the energy of Expressionism and the bright colors of the Fauvists. He wanted to convey traditional themes to modern audiences. Thompson said of his paintings, "The monsters are present now on my canvas as in my dreams." He died just before his twenty-ninth birthday but created more than a thousand paintings in his short life.

 **Thomas Hart Benton** (1889–1975) was raised in a political family in Missouri, then spent time in Washington, DC. Thomas was a good harmonica player and loved drawing. His first job was as a staff artist at a newspaper, where he drew cartoons. After studying painting in New York and Paris, he returned to Missouri and began painting in an American Regionalist style, recording life in the Midwest. Heroic figures are a hallmark of his art. Benton was socially conscious and did not shy away from painting the racism and poverty he saw around him. Benton said of his work, "If it's not art, it's at least history."

 **Henri de Toulouse-Lautrec** (1864–1901) was born into an aristocratic family in France. As a child, he spent time painting and drawing because his health limited his activity. Henri suffered from a genetic disorder that made his bones fragile and stunted his growth. His legs always bothered him, and he walked with a cane. When trying to paint landscapes at age fifteen, Henri

told a friend, "I am quite incapable of doing them . . . . My trees look like spinach and my sea like heaven knows what." Moving to Montmartre in Paris, Henri painted the artists, entertainers, and carousers there, developing his Post-Impressionist style. Toulouse-Lautrec is known for his posters and printmaking, including *Moulin Rouge: La Goulue*. (The Moulin Rouge was a famous Parisian cabaret, and La Goulue was the stage name of dancer Louise Weber.)

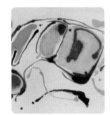 **Helen Frankenthaler** (1928–2011) grew up in Manhattan's Upper East Side, absorbing the New York art scene. She was not afraid to take artistic risks. After seeing Jackson Pollock's drip style, Helen developed her own staining technique for painting. She used oil paint thinned with turpentine to make washes on unprimed canvas. Helen painted wonderful colors on large canvases placed on the floor so she could move around a painting and interact with it. She wanted her art to feel spontaneous. During her long career, Helen created pieces reflecting Cubism, Abstract Expressionism, and Color Field painting. She advised beginners, "Challenge yourself. The worst is it looks awful, but it might look wonderful and surprise you." It is evident from her paintings that Helen continued challenging herself throughout her career.

 **Claude Monet** (1840–1926) grew up in the port city of Le Havre, France, where he drew charcoal caricatures and sold them to people in town. Monet loved painting outside. He used short brush strokes and bright colors to capture the light and movement of nature on canvas. After moving to Paris, Monet became one of the founders of Impressionism. He said, "When you go out to paint, try to forget what objects you have before you, a tree, a house, a field or whatever. Merely think here is a little square of blue, here an oblong of pink, here a streak of yellow, and paint it just as it looks to you . . . until it gives your … impression of the scene before you." Monet made many paintings in his lifetime, including over two hundred and fifty paintings of waterlilies.

Greg Newbold's Advice for Artists

Developing your unique artistic style and voice
takes work, so keep practicing. Here are three tips:

1. Draw.

Drawing is magic, and it's the best way to improve your art. Try to draw exactly what you see. Look for big shapes before you add details. Draw an object from different angles to develop perspective. Carry a sketchbook and draw all the time. Once you can draw realistically, you will be able to make real objects look however you want. Simplify shapes. Stylize and distort things. Merge objects for fun.

2. Explore.

Artists undertake long journeys to discover their styles. On your journey, experiment with acrylic paints, watercolors, charcoals, pastel chalks, colored pencils, or oil paints. Try surfaces like paper, canvas, cardboard, metal, or wood. Combine materials and methods to find out how they respond to each other. Maybe you will like painting on collaged magazine clippings or printed fabric. Glue objects into your art and paint around or on top of them.

3. Have Fun!

With each color or brush stroke you apply, let the picture suggest what to do next. Trust your vision. There is no right or wrong way to make art, only ways that work or don't work. If your picture doesn't turn out quite the way you wanted, figure out what worked well and use that knowledge in the future. Be inspired by other artists, but don't compare your work with theirs. They are not you!

Good luck on your artistic journey!

Photo by Kelly Price

As a child, AMY NEWBOLD played monster games with her siblings in the backyard. She learned to read at age four and wrote her first monster story in the second grade. Besides writing, Amy also loves to draw and paint and looks forward to trying new painting styles. Although she once fell asleep in art history class, she has always loved art, museums, and museum gift shops. Amy enjoys road trips, hiking in the mountains near her Utah home, and really good chocolate.

GREG NEWBOLD loved to draw and paint as a child. He and his siblings often created giant scenes on rolls of newsprint spread on the unfinished basement floor. Greg watched every science fiction and monster movie he could find, and he loved the movie monsters coloring book he bought at an elementary school book fair. As an award-winning illustrator, he now gets to create his own creatures and especially enjoys making picture books with his wife, Amy. Greg likes gardening, fishing, daydreaming, and painting anything amazing he encounters on road trips with his wife and family.

If you've enjoyed this book, don't miss its companions!

AMY & GREG NEWBOLD

If *Picasso* painted a SNOWMAN

$17.95 hardcover • 978-088448-593-3

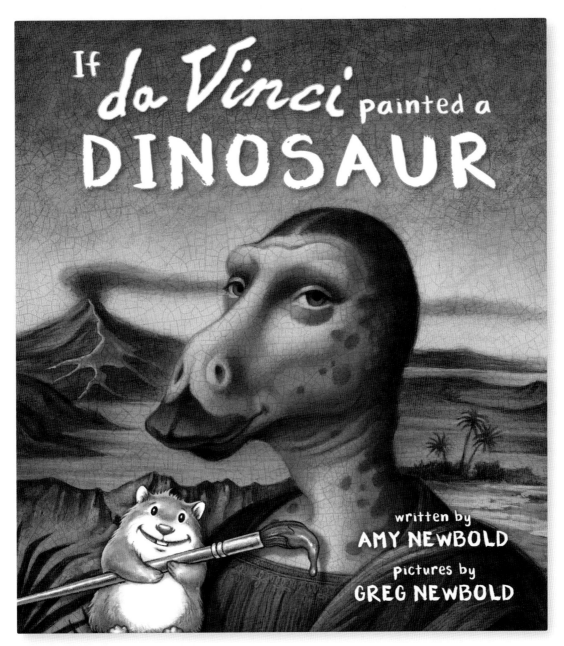

If *da Vinci* painted a DINOSAUR

written by
AMY NEWBOLD

pictures by
GREG NEWBOLD

"Art history with a little smile."
—*Kirkus Reviews*

"A memorable introduction
to famed works of art."
—*Publishers Weekly*

"An obvious choice
for young art
enthusiasts."
—*School Library Journal*

$17.95 hardcover • 978-088448-667-1

For my dad, in loving memory.
—A.N.

For my kids, who have explored countless art museums with me.
—G.N

Tilbury House Publishers
12 Starr Street
Thomaston, Maine 04861
www.tilburyhouse.com

Text © 2019 by Amy Newbold
Illustrations © 2019 by Greg Newbold

Hardcover ISBN 978-088448-768-5
ebook ISBN 978-0-88448-770-8

First hardcover printing September 2019

15 16 17 18 19 20 XXX 10 9 8 7 6 5 4 3 2 1

Library of Congress Control Number: 2019940803

Designed by Frame25 Productions
Printed in Korea